PISTOL

PACKIN'

PREACHER!

Johnny A Palmer Jr.

Content:

Introduction

As the song goes, "You don't tug on Superman's cape; You don't spit into the wind; You don't pull the mask off that ole Lone Ranger - And you don't mess around with John Wayne!" Well, not exactly, but John Wayne is one of my hero's. I think we could use a few more Christian type John Wayne's out there. It seems every time you turn on the TV there is another shooting. Now it seems to be fashionable to shoot up churches. Not long ago, we all read about 26 people killed in a shooting at a church down in Texas.[1] The weird thing is that most Christians seem to think it is Biblical to put a bulls-eye on their church and say come on in and blast away, we will not resist you.

One John Wayne movie, Big Jake', in a scene where he is talking to his son Michael:

Well, Michael,
you were supposed to shoot.
With this?
It's a gun, isn't it?

---

[1] cnn.com/2017/11/05/us/texas-church-shooting/index.html

Well, yes, of course.
Well, shoot it.
But, Father...
(The scene shows his son using a gas-
operated gun with more than six shots.
He is shooting wildly).
Boy, you need a keeper.
Pa, I wouldn't
come out just yet.
Sam, I want to offer
my personal apologies.
You can get up now.
I'm not coming out.
Not till you say
I can shoot back.[2]

I think it's time we let those who think
the church is an easy target know that
according to the Word of God we can
shoot back! No, we are not itching for a
fight; we rather welcome them to come
and hear the gospel and be saved.

Now, lest you think I am new at this, let
me say that I was saved on May 7,
1974. Glorious day! I was Licensed to
preach in 1977 and later ordained. I
now pastor my third church and have

[2] www.springfieldspringfield.co.uk/movie_script.php?movie=big-jake.

been here over 32 years. So I am not exactly a newly planted preacher! After hearing about a church where a man killed several members I decided that if they shoot at my members – I am going to stop them, Lord willing, before they wipe our little church out. So I got a concealed weapon permit, bought a gun, and wear it behind the pulpit every Sunday. But the question is, is this Biblical. I have built my entire ministry on a verse by verse preaching of the Bible and a deep desire to give all the glory to the Lord Jesus Christ. So, this book is a result of my Biblical search for an answer to whether it is right in the eyes of the Lord to protect the people that He has entrusted to my care. Keep an open mind, that is a mind open to what the Bible has to say on the subject, and let's get going – we're burning daylight!

Chapter One

Turning the other Cheek

Turn the other cheek — The rule of thumb when the other guy is bigger.

Whoever hits you on the cheek, offer him the other also; and whoever takes away your coat, do not withhold your shirt from him either. Luke 6:29

Explanation:

But I say to you, do not resist an evil person; but whoever slaps you on your right cheek, turn the other to him also. Matthew 5: 39

About 90% of people in the world are right handed. They slap people using their right hand. But if you slap somebody using you right hand, you will hit their left cheek. If you slap somebody with your right hand you will miss their right cheek altogether! Therefore, it is likely that he is talking figurative not literally. He is talking about being insulted.

Experts:

Robinson notes, "Jesus was not speaking literally. He was talking about insults at us, not muggers in the subway!"

John Stott, "Christ's illustrations are not to be taken as the charter for any unscrupulous tyrant, beggar, or thug. His purpose was to forbid revenge, not to encourage injustice, dishonesty or vice. True love takes action to deter evil and to promote good. He teaches not the irresponsibility which encourages evil but the forbearance which renounces revenge."

Martin Luther, "Some crazy saints would let mice nibble at them and refuse to kill any of them on account of this text maintaining that he had to suffer and could not resist evil."

Swindoll, "If you have roaches or mice, don't twist Jesus words into a persuasive plea for letting them live on, untouched. Likewise, if you have rats – poison the suckers! Furthermore, if our nation encounters an enemy who would steal our liberty there is nothing in this that even implies we should let that enemy conquer us.

It is true we can all quote from many so-called experts and come up with a variety of opinions that leave us scratching our heads. It reminds me of a census taker who knocked on the door of a backwoods shack. A fellow came to the door. "The president has sent us across the country to find out how many people live in the United States." The man replied. "I'm sorry you came all the way out here to ask me, 'cause I ain't got the faintest idea." But it still is helpful in that there is wisdom in a multitude of counsel (Prov. 11:14).

The only real Expert: The Lord Jesus Christ!

Hal Roach, film and TV director, had a reputation for spotting talent. He spotted such talents as Will Rogers, Laurel and Hardy, Harold Lloyd, Charlie Chase, Harry Langdon, and those kids of the Our Gang and Little Rascals series. But every human expert gets it wrong from time to time. Hal actually turned away Mickey Rooney and Shirley Temple! Therefore we must turn to the only expert who gets it right 100%, 24/7.

A Consideration of Jesus' actions.

When Jesus was literally punched, he did not, turn the other cheek. He responded!

22 When He had said this, one of the officers standing nearby struck Jesus, saying, "Is that the way You answer the high priest?" 23 Jesus answered him, "If I have spoken wrongly, testify of the wrong; but if rightly, why do you strike Me?" John 18: 22-23

Most view our Lord as a pacifist who never used any form of violence, but that is not really true.

13 The Passover of the Jews was near, and Jesus went up to Jerusalem. 14 And He found in the temple those who were selling oxen and sheep and doves, and the money changers seated at their tables. 15 And He made a scourge of cords, and drove them all out of the temple, with the sheep and the oxen; and He poured out the coins of the money changers and overturned their tables; 16 and to those who were selling the doves He said, "Take these things away; stop making My Father's house a place of business." 17 His disciples remembered that it was written, "ZEAL FOR YOUR HOUSE WILL CONSUME ME." John 2:13-17

It is of course true that our Lord was gentle, but that did not rule out the fact that He was also judgmental.

Gentle Jesus, meek and mild, is a concept that has been so overworked that many today preach and follow a Christ who has no resemblance to the Christ of the New Testament. That Jesus is an idol, drained of his true deity—a weak, good-natured deity whose great aim is to let us off the hook.
Do not get me wrong. Jesus *is* meek and mild. In fact, he describes himself in that way in Matthew 11:29 when he invites those who have burdens to come to him. Dozens of Scriptures in the New Testament testify to his gentleness. But we need to balance this with other descriptions of our Lord. For instance, in Mark 3:5, the passage describing the man with the paralyzed hand, Jesus looked around at all those who were questioning whether or not he would heal on the Sabbath, and "he looked

around at them in anger." Jesus' anger was a swelling wrath. There was nothing gentle in the fierce message he sent to Herod either: "Go tell that fox..." (Luke 13:32), or in his response to Peter: "Out of my sight, Satan!" (Matthew 16:23). I am sure the Pharisees in the temple saw nothing of his gentleness, meekness, and mildness when he said, "You are like whitewashed tombs" (Matthew 23:27) and "You snakes! You brood of vipers. How will you escape being condemned to hell?" (Matthew 23:33). The scene described in our text is a wild scene! Men were grasping at their moneybags and tables as Jesus applied the whip to those not moving.

But the fact is, Jesus was as Godlike here as he was when he hung on the cross. He was revealing as much of God on this occasion as he did at Calvary. He was displaying a great underlying truth: Love presupposes hatred. A love for the downtrodden, the poor, and the oppressed also brings about a hatred for the conditions that caused their suffering. That truth has been evident in the lives of Shaftesbury, the Wesleys, Fox, and other great men of the church down through the centuries. Men and women of great love have always also been people of great hatred. In fact, you can tell as much about a person by his hatreds as by his loves. So what has been revealed through Christ's anger is very important. What are the hates and loves of God? In particular, what is the root of Christ's hatred and anger in this passage? And how should it affect our lives?[3]

Some time we do act a little silly, we are not talking about getting even or revenge but self-defense. I couldn't help but thinking of something I read the other day. Jane Vajnar shared this:

My friend's four boys were young and bursting with energy, especially in church. But the sermon her minister preached on "turning the other cheek" got their undivided attention. The minister stressed that no matter what others do to us, we should never try to "get even." That afternoon the youngest

[3] R. Kent Hughes, *Preaching the Word – John: That You May Believe*, (Wheaton, IL: Crossway Books, 1999), WORD*search* CROSS e-book, 67-68.

boy came into the house crying. Between sobs he told his mother he had kicked one of his brothers, who had kicked him in return. "I'm sorry you're hurt," his mother said. "But you shouldn't go around kicking people." To which the tearful child replied, "But the preacher said he isn't supposed to kick me back."[4]

Chapter Two

Carrying a Concealed weapon?

Johnny Cash made this comment before singing 'Ragged Old Flag':

I love the freedoms we have in this country. I appreciate your right to burn your flag if you want too. But I really appreciate my right to bear arms so I can shoot you if you try to burn mine.

Of course, we are not taking about shooting someone for trying to destroy our property as much as for defending our life and the lives of others.

John MacArthur notes:

---

[4] Jane Vajnar, Tampa, Kansas. "Lite Fare," Christian Reader.

The command, whoever hits you on the cheek, offer him the other also does not preclude the self-defense mechanisms God has provided for self-preservation. Jesus was not forbidding His followers to defend themselves if they were dangerously attacked. In Luke 22: 36 He instructed the apostles to buy a sword for protection if they did not have one.[5]

Now this brings us to the question of defending the flock. What if someone came in and started shooting people this morning? At Emanuel African Methodist Episcopal Church, back in June 2015, Dylann Roof murdered 9 members of that church. Recently justice was served as he received the death penalty. Many big churches have security guards or police in attendance, a small church like ours does not have the means for such security. If somebody came in and murdered nine of us there wouldn't be much of a church left! Can we defend ourselves if confronted with such a situation?

---

[5] MacArthur, John F.. Luke 1-24 MacArthur New Testament Commentary Set (MacArthur New Testament).

Chapter Three

Considering something more authoritative than the NRA

Billy Graham was right:

As Christians, we have only one authority, one compass: the Word of God.[6]

Well, let's look at what the Bible says about self-defense.

- [2] *"If the thief is caught while breaking in and is struck so that he dies, there will be no bloodguiltiness on his account.* [3] *"But if the sun has risen on him, there will be bloodguiltiness on his account. He shall surely make restitution; if he owns nothing, then he shall be sold for his theft. Exodus 22:2-3*

  J. Vernon McGee notes, "This law gives you the right to self-protection. Not long ago, a thief broke into a man's place and the homeowner shot

---

[6] Billy Graham, The Secret of Happiness (New York: Doubleday, 1955), 153.

him. He sued the homeowner for several thousand dollars in damages. The case went to court and the thief won the judgment on the grounds that the homeowner had no right to shoot him, according to the decision of some asinine judge! In order to pay the damages the homeowner had to sell his property. And there was no judgment against the thief at all! In our day, there is a great emphasis on protecting the rights of the guilty at the expense of the rights of the innocent. God's law protects a man's property and his home. Under this principle a man is justified in protecting his property, his home, and his loved ones."[7]

Adrian Rogers writes, "Now, what does that mean? It means that if, in the middle of the night, you wake up and there's someone breaking in your door—you can't see who it is; the sun is not up; you don't know what he has in

---

[7] McGee, J. Vernon. Thru the Bible Commentary, Volumes 1-5: Genesis through Revelation (Kindle Location 11131). Thomas Nelson. Kindle Edition.

mind; you're afraid for life and limb—
and, in your attempt to protect yourself
or the life of your loved ones, that
man's life is taken, God says you are
not held accountable... If you kill
someone breaking into your home, and
you don't know but what he may mean
to maim your wife, or rape your
daughter, or you don't know what is
happening, and you, in the middle of
the night, are protecting your own life,
your own loved ones, and— the Bible
says— he's breaking in, then God does
not hold you culpable. God does not
hold you accountable."[8]

PS: This in the context looks like it's
talking about protecting livestock. What
is a person doing sleeping with the
livestock? The truth is that often the
livestock stayed at night in the home.
So in essence, this is a home invasion.

- [8] *"Now you write to the Jews as
  you see fit, in the king's name, and
  seal it with the king's signet ring;*

[8] Adrian Rogers, *The Adrian Rogers Legacy Collection – Sermons*,
(North Palm Beach, FL: Adrian Rogers Foundation, 2011), WORD*search*
CROSS e-book, Under: "The Sixth Commandment".

for a decree which is written in the name of the king and sealed with the king's signet ring may not be revoked." ⁹ So the king's scribes were called at that time in the third month (that is, the month Sivan), on the twenty-third day; and it was written according to all that Mordecai commanded to the Jews, the satraps, the governors and the princes of the provinces which extended from India to Ethiopia, 127 provinces, to every province according to its script, and to every people according to their language as well as to the Jews according to their script and their language. ¹⁰He wrote in the name of King Ahasuerus, and sealed it with the king's signet ring, and sent letters by couriers on horses, riding on steeds sired by the royal stud. ¹¹ In them the king granted the Jews who were in each and every city the right to assemble and to defend their lives, to destroy, to kill and to annihilate the entire army of any people or province which might attack them, including children and women, and to plunder their spoil, Esther 8:8-11

Haman manipulated the king into passing a law declaring that on a certain day it would be "open season" on the Jews; when the king realized that Haman had manipulated him, he passed a second law granting the Jews the right to defend themselves from the scheduled attack. Thus the Jews struck all their enemies:

5 Thus the Jews struck all their enemies with the sword, killing and destroying; and they did what they pleased to those who hated them. Esther 9:5

These were Jewish citizens, not police or military folks, and yet, they had the right to defend themselves.

- *11 Our enemies said, "They will not know or see until we come among them, kill them and put a stop to the work." 12 When the Jews who lived near them came and told us ten times, "They will come up against us from every place where you may turn," 13 then I stationed*

men in the lowest parts of the space behind the wall, the exposed places, and I stationed the people in families with their swords, spears and bows. 14 When I saw their fear, I rose and spoke to the nobles, the officials and the rest of the people: "Do not be afraid of them; remember the Lord who is great and awesome, and fight for your brothers, your sons, your daughters, your wives and your houses." 15 When our enemies heard that it was known to us, and that God had frustrated their plan, then all of us returned to the wall, each one to his work. 16 From that day on, half of my servants carried on the work while half of them held the spears, the shields, the bows and the breastplates; and the captains were behind the whole house of Judah. 17 Those who were rebuilding the wall and those who carried burdens took their load with one hand doing the work and the other holding a weapon.
Nehemiah 4:11-17

Nehemiah was returning to Israel from Persian exile to lead the effort to rebuild the walls of Jerusalem. Because of the violent opposition, he instructs them to be ready to defend themselves. Notice verse 20, he did not see any inconsistency between them arming themselves and trusting God to fight for them.

20 *"At whatever place you hear the sound of the trumpet, rally to us there. Our God will fight for us."*
Nehemiah 4:20

- 35 *And He said to them, "When I sent you out without money belt and bag and sandals, you did not lack anything, did you?" They said, "No, nothing." 36 And He said to them, "But now, whoever has a money belt is to take it along, likewise also a bag, and whoever has no sword is to sell his coat and buy one. 37 "For I tell you that this which is written must be fulfilled in Me, 'AND HE WAS NUMBERED WITH TRANSGRESSORS'; for that which refers to Me has its*

fulfillment." 38 They said, "Lord, look, here are two swords." And He said to them, "It is enough."
Luke 22:35-38

We already looked at this. St. Cyril of Alexandria (c. 376-444 AD) said this about Luke 22: 36:

The saying in appearance had reference to the apostles but in reality applied to every Jew [every believer in Jesus Christ]. Christ addressed them. He did not say that the holy apostles must get a purse and bag. He said that whosoever has a purse [money], let him take it. This means that whoever had property in the Jewish territories should collect all that he had and [be ready to] flee, so that he could save himself, he might do so. Some not having the means of equipping themselves for travel [escape and/ or self-defense], and from extreme poverty must continue in the land (area of conflict / location of danger]. 'Let such a person,' Jesus says, 'sell his cloak and buy a sword.' From now on, the question with all those who continue in the land will not be whether they possess anything or not, but whether they can exist [without a sword] and preserve their lives.[9]

St. Ambrose of Milan (c. 340-397 AD), said this about the supposed dichotomy of Jesus' teaching on this subject:

Why do you [Jesus] who forbid me to wield a sword now command me to buy one? Why do you command me to have what you [previously] forbid me to draw? Perhaps He may command this so that a defense may be prepared, not as a necessary revenge, but that you may be seen to have been able to be avenged but to be unwilling to take revenge. [In regard to self-defense], the law does not forbid me to strike back [when being attacked]...This seems wicked to many, but the Lord is not wicked, He [Jesus] who when he could take revenge chose to be sacrificed."[10]

1 Tim. 5: 8 – part of what we provide for our family is protection.

---

[9] St. Cyril of Alexandria (c. 376-444 AD); Commentary on Luke, Homily 145, GGSL 579.

[10] St. Ambrose; Exposition of the Gospel of Luke; 10.53-55, EHG 405-6.

Objections: Jn. 18:10-11

10 Simon Peter then, having a sword, drew it and struck the high priest's slave, and cut off his right ear; and the slave's name was Malchus. 11 So Jesus said to Peter, "Put the sword into the sheath; the cup which the Father has given Me, shall I not drink it?"
John 18:10-11

Peter carried a concealed weapon, [A sword, usually carried in a sheath hung from the belt, was the handgun of Jesus' day. It was more about 18 inches, more of what we would call a deadly knife today] the rebuke was not because Peter had a sword but it was his inappropriate use of his sword on this occasion. It was God's will for Jesus to be apprehended and crucified. Let me say, if it is God's will that we suffer martyrdom for Christ, then we should gladly give our lives for Him. If someone puts a gun to my head and says deny Christ or I will shoot – I say "Shoot away!" But that is not the same thing as allowing a burglar to break into your house and shoot you and your family.

What glory does that bring to the Lord Jesus Christ?

One objects, I trust God! The question is can we not trust God and use common sense? Those who say they trust God are the same ones who believe in having a strong military. Those who say I trust God still call 911 in an emergency and want the police to protect them. It reminds me of one, who when asked why he carried a concealed weapon, said, "Because I can't carry a police officer." Those who say that they trust God still lock their doors at night and their cars when they go somewhere. The truth is we can trust God and use reasonable means in life. Side note: Today there are "Stand Your Ground" laws in some states, where when your life is threatened you can defend yourself.

The fatal shooting of Trayvon Martin by George Zimmerman took place on the night of February 26, 2012, in Sanford, Florida. Six weeks later, amid widespread, intense and contradictory media coverage, a special prosecutor appointed by Governor Rick Scott charged Zimmerman with murder. Zimmerman's trial began on June 10, 2013, in Sanford. On July 13, 2013, a jury acquitted him of second-degree murder and of manslaughter charges. The states that have legislatively adopted stand-your-ground laws are: Alabama, Alaska, Arizona, Arkansas, California, Florida, Georgia, Indiana, Kansas, Kentucky, Louisiana, Maine, Michigan, Mississippi, Missouri, Montana, New Hampshire, North Carolina (Stand Your Ground law (N.C.G.S. 14 51.3), North Dakota, Oklahoma, Pennsylvania, South Carolina, South Dakota, Tennessee, Texas, Utah, West Virginia, Wisconsin, and Wyoming. Other states (Iowa, Virginia, and Washington) have considered stand-your-ground laws of their own. "Arkansans can use deadly force if they believe someone is about to commit a violent felony or about to use deadly force against them. Force can also be used if there is a pattern of domestic abuse that the victim feels may be life-threatening." So we have both a Biblical and Constitutional right to bear arms:

The 2nd Amendment says, "the right of the people to keep and bear Arms, shall not be infringed," Our Forefathers knew that when citizens are unarmed both Government and Criminals become oppressive and dangerous.

Noah Webster, Founding Father:

Before a standing army can rule, the people must be disarmed; as they are in almost every kingdom in Europe. The supreme power in America cannot enforce unjust laws by the sword; because the whole body of the people are armed, and constitute a force superior to any band of regular troops that can be, on any pretence, raised in the United States. A military force, at the command of Congress, can execute no laws, but such as the people perceive to be just and constitutional; for they will possess the power.

Thomas Jefferson:

Laws that forbid the carrying of arms. . . disarm only those who are neither inclined nor determined to commit crimes. . . Such laws make things worse for the assaulted and better for the assailants; they serve rather to encourage than to prevent homicides, for an unarmed man may be attacked with greater confidence than an armed man.

Alexander Hamilton:

If circumstances should at any time oblige the government to form an army of any magnitude, that army can never be formidable to the liberties of the people while there is a large body of citizens, little if at all inferior to them in discipline and the use of arms, who stand ready to defend their rights and those of their fellow citizens.

Today gun control is not about public safety but government control. As the saying goes, "When guns are outlawed, only outlaws have guns.

One noted:

If gun control worked, then Chicago and Washington, D.C. would be the safest cities in the country. These cities have had the strictest 'gun control' laws for many years, yet they also have the highest crime rates. When we compare the crime in these cities to other communities which have scrapped their anti-gun laws and have made concealed carry of a handgun legal, we observe that more guns actually result in less crime.

What about being submissive to the Government, yes that is a Biblical commandment but as long as America is built on "We the people..." and we have a right to vote in or out government that is ungodly and against the people, we have an obligation to make our voices heard. I suspect that is part of the reason why Donald Trump won the election. That does not mean our hope is in good government but it is in almighty God, who has promised to rapture us out of here, but until He does we have to live in this sick and violent world. Keep in mind we are NOT talking about revenge or being vengeful or trigger happy but self-defense when there is no other option. Note, if someone shoots one of your children, you have no right to track them down and kill them; but if you are there when someone is trying to shoot one of your children you do have a right to defend them.

We should ask:

Would a reasonable person consider this situation a threat to their life? We are not talking about using deadly force against one who is giving us a tongue-lashing. Is the threat credible, does the person have the means to carry out bodily harm. Or am I overreacting in a panic mode. Is there a possible way out other then self-defense? Can you call 911, or run to a place of safety, etc. Am I still reacting after the threat is over? If someone is seeking to do you harm and you pull out a weapon and they then take off, the threat is over. There is no justification for shooting after the danger is over! If someone breaks into my house and I confront them with a gun and they take off, I have no reason to shoot them in the back as they are fleeing.

Chapter Four

What if they carry me out feet first?

Let me ask you one of the most important questions you will ever ponder.

Have you come to a place in your life where you know for certain that if you died you would go to heaven?

The only answer to that question is, yes, no, or I don't know. Take a moment and think about it. A follow up question would be:'

If you were standing before God right now and He were to ask, "Why should I let you into my perfect heaven?"

What do you think you would say? You might say, "I go to church. I try to live a good life. I try to keep God's law." Such responses are sincere, and I appreciate your honesty. Most would probably say, "I don't know what I would say." Well, would you like to know? Then read the following carefully.

God Really Does Love You

"For God so loved the world, (put your name here), that He gave His only begotten Son, that whoever believes in Him should not perish but have everlasting life" (John 3:16).

It is natural to question this claim; we tend to wonder how God could love us with all of our problems and hang-ups, yes, you can say it – with all of our sins. My wife and I have had two children. When they were born they did nothing for us! And after they were born, for the first several months they kept us up all hours of the night; we had to change their diapers and feed them. I think most of you know what I'm talking about. However, we did love them. Why? I suppose it was because we had something to do with them being in this world. They are our children; they even looked a little like us – poor kids! You need to realize that God is the one who had everything to do with your coming into this world. Without God you would not even exist! He is the Creator and Sustainer of life. He, in fact, created you in His image and loves you even though you have done nothing to deserve it.

So What's a Fella to Do?

Have you ever felt that your life lacked purpose and meaning? Have these thoughts ever crossed your mind:

- Where did I come from?
- Why am I here?
- Where am I going?

God knows the answer to these questions. He created you with a definite purpose in mind.

"The thief does not come except to steal, and to kill, and to destroy. I have come that they may have life, and that they may have it more abundantly" (John 10:10).

An abundant life is a life of purpose, meaning, and fulfillment. That is what God offers you. This brings up an unavoidable question—what happened! If He loves us and has this great purpose for our life, then why are both concepts so foreign to us? The answer is both profound and very simple.

Sin Separates!

We are all sinners, "for all have sinned and fall short of the glory of God" (Rom. 3:22). We are a sinner by birth. God created Adam and Eve and put them in a garden with only one commandment; they were not to eat of a certain tree. They disobeyed God by taking a bite, and thus they sinned. Now what kind of babies are two sinful people capable of having? It is the law of biogenesis—like produces like. This is why there is no need to teach children how to tell a lie, but only to teach them positive things like telling the truth. They know how to lie naturally!
The reason for that is that we are all born with a sin nature inherited from Adam.

"Therefore, just as through one man sin entered the world, and death through sin, and thus death spread to all men, because all sinned" (Rom. 5:12).

We are also sinners by behavior. Have you not sinned? The Bible commands us to love God with all our heart, mind, and soul. Have you always done that? Have you ever done that? Have you ever told a lie? Have you ever wanted to? God not only looks at our deeds but at our desires. The Bible clearly declares we have all sinned.

So What?

Here is the answer to the so-what question.

"For the wages of sin is death, but the gift of God is eternal life in Christ Jesus our Lord" (Rom. 6:23).

What we have earned from our sin is death. Death means separation.

- There is spiritual death—the separation of the spirit/soul from God. "And the LORD God commanded the man, saying, 'Of every tree of the garden you may freely eat; but of the tree of the knowledge of good and evil you shall not eat, for in the day that you eat of it you shall surely die'"

(Gen. 2:16–17). The day they ate of it they did not physically die; that took place many years later. But God said *in the day* you eat of it you will die. They died spiritually that very day.

- There is also physical death—the separation of the spirit/soul from the body. "And as it is appointed for men to die once, but after this the judgment" (Heb. 9:27). The fact that everybody dies physically is proof positive that everyone is spiritually dead. If we were not sinners, we would not die. The statistics are rather impressive; one out of every one person dies!

- If you die physically while you are spiritually dead, you will die eternally. Eternal death is the eternal separation of the spirit/soul/body from God's goodness, grace, mercy, and blessings. It is to be fully conscious and live in a place the Bible calls the lake of fire. "Then Death and Hades were cast into the lake of fire. This is the second death. And anyone not found written in the Book of Life was cast into the lake of fire" (Rev. 20:14–15).

Question: How can you say one moment that God loves me and then in the next that He condemns me?

Well let us imagine putting on a judge's robe and sitting on the bench. Then the unthinkable happens. Your son, whom you love very much, is brought before you, guilty of a capital offense! The penalty for his crime is death, and the evidence is clear as to his guilt. Would you sentence him to death? If you were a just judge, you would, not because you no longer love him, but in spite of your great love for him. God is holy, righteous, and just, as well as a God of love. This looks like bad news! However, the very word *gospel* means good news, so where is this good news?

Jesus Christ Is God

"In the beginning was the Word, and the Word was with God, and the Word was God" (John 1:1).

This is a great mystery, but the Bible teaches that God became God/man. "And the Word became flesh and dwelt among us, and we beheld His glory, the glory as of the only begotten of the Father, full of grace and truth" (John 1:14).

Jesus Christ the Substitute

The Lord Jesus Christ lived a perfect life and then died in your place. "But God demonstrates His own love toward us, in that while we were still sinners, Christ died for us" (Rom. 5:8 NKJV).

Let us put our judge robe back on for a minute. Imagine after sentencing your boy to be executed, taking off your robe and then voluntarily offering to die in his place. That would make you just and loving at the same time. That is what Jesus Christ actually did for us. We do not understand all of this but must accept it by faith. I do not understand electricity, but I still do not live in the dark. I do not understand how the digestive system works, but I still eat. I do not understand how a brown cow eats green grass and produces white milk. You do not have to understand everything to be saved—just that you are a sinner and that Jesus Christ died for your sin.

He Is Not Here, He Has Risen

"For I delivered to you first of all that which I also received: that Christ died for our sins according to the Scriptures, and that He was buried, and that He rose again the third day according to the Scriptures, and that He was seen by Cephas, then by the twelve. After that He was seen by over five hundred brethren at once, of whom the greater part remain to the present, but some have fallen asleep" (1 Cor. 15:3–6).

By rising from the dead, He proved that He paid for all of our sins. If He had not, death would have held Him. It also proved that He had no sin of His own. If

He had, He would have stayed dead like everybody else.

One Way Only

We have all seen *One Way Only* signs, and so it is with the way of salvation. There is only one person who can save. "Jesus said to him, 'I am the way, the truth, and the life. No one comes to the Father except through Me'" (John 14:6).

You can line up every one of us on the West Coast with plans to swim to Hawaii, and no doubt, some would swim a lot farther than others. Nevertheless, we would all have one thing in common: nobody would make it! It is impossible for anybody to swim from the West Coast to Hawaii. And it is just as impossible for sinful man to make his way to a Holy God on his own without experiencing God's wrath. What one needs is a boat to get them from the West Coast to Hawaii. Moreover, the only salvation boat is the Lord Jesus Christ. That Jesus is the only way to be saved is as true as $2 + 2 = 4$. There is only one answer to that equation, and there is only one way to be saved.

"Nor is there salvation in any other, for there is no other name under heaven given among men by which we must be saved" (Acts 4:12).

Facts

These are only facts. Giving mental assent to these facts is not enough to save anyone. It is not enough to give intellectual assent to these facts. We must believe and thus receive Christ.

"But as many as received Him, to them He gave the right to become children of God, to those who believe in His name" (John 1:12).

Faith

Facts must be wedded to faith. So, what do we mean when we say believe or place your faith in Christ?

Faith involves mind, emotion, and will.

Years ago, a tightrope walker named Charles Blondin, went across Niagara Falls, walking on a wire. He went back and forth. He even filled a wheelbarrow with bricks and took that across. A crowd gathered, and he asked one of them, "Do you believe I could do that with you?" The man agreed that he could. Then Blondin said, "Hop on in, and I'll carry you across." The man said, "No way!" You see, he did not really believe. He believed in his mind that Blondin could take him across; he wanted him to in his emotions, but he would not commit himself to Blondin and trust him to take him across. Saving faith involves our mind, emotion, and will.

Amazing Grace

You likely have heard the song, "Amazing Grace." We are saved by grace through faith in Jesus Christ. Now faith is not a work—faith is to believe in the work of another. "For by grace you have been saved through faith, and that not of yourselves; it is the gift of

God, not of works, lest anyone should boast" (Eph. 2:8–9).

Dr. Gerstner: "Christ has done everything necessary for his salvation. Nothing now stands between the sinner and God but the sinner's good works. Nothing can keep him from Christ but his delusion that he does not need Him—that he has good works of his own that can satisfy God. If men will only be convinced that all their righteousness is as filthy rags; if men will see that there is none that does good, no, not one; if men will see that all are shut up under sin—then there will be nothing to prevent their everlasting salvation. All they need is need. All they must have is nothing. All that is required is acknowledged guilt. But alas, sinners cannot part from their virtues. They are imaginary, but they are real to them. So grace becomes unreal. The real grace of God they spurn in order to hold on to the illusory virtues of their own. Their eyes fixed on a mirage; they will not drink real water. They die of thirst in the midst of an ocean of grace."

Repentance is a synonym for faith; it is like heads and tails of *one* coin. Repentance is not making a vow you will stop sinning, nor is it a change of life. You cannot stop sinning or change your life until God saves you! I have fished most of my life and I have never cleaned a fish before I caught it. Repentance is a *change of mind*, about who you are, a sinner; and about the Lord Jesus Christ, the only one who can save you based on His death, burial, and resurrection.

Good Enough Is Not Good Enough

The religious leaders of Jesus' day prayed three times a week, fasted twice a week, never missed going to the house of worship, and memorized the Old Testament (Luke 18:9–12). Yet, Jesus said that if you are not more righteous then they, you are not going to make it!

"For I say to you, that unless your righteousness exceeds the righteousness of the scribes and

Pharisees, you will by no means enter the kingdom of heaven (Matt. 5:20).

Then he says something rather startling:

"Therefore you shall be perfect, just as your Father in heaven is perfect" (Matt. 5:48).

Did you know Jesus said it takes perfect righteousness to get to heaven? We all know that nobody is perfect! How then can we be perfectly righteous before a perfectly righteous God?

"For He made Him who knew no sin to be sin for us, that we might become the righteousness of God in Him" (2 Cor. 5:21).

The truth is, there is only one person who lived a perfect life, and that was Jesus Christ. You see, the good news is that not only did Jesus die on the cross in our place, to offer us forgiveness of all our sins, He also offers us His perfect righteousness, placed on our account! The only sin Jesus ever knew was ours;

the only righteousness we will ever know is His.

Never the Same!

Salvation is not an external thing. When you receive Jesus Christ as your Savior, He makes you a new creature within!

"Therefore, if anyone is in Christ, he is a new creation; old things have passed away; behold, all things have become new" (2 Cor. 5:17).

And the Holy Spirit takes up permanent residence within you.

"And because you are sons, God has sent forth the Spirit of His Son into your hearts, crying out, 'Abba, Father'" (Gal. 4:6).

Thus, you now have the desire (new nature) and the power (indwelling Holy Spirit) to live for God. You are positionally changed from being in Adam to now being in Christ, and experientially changed because the inner transformation of regeneration and salvation begins the process of progressive sanctification, which ultimately leads to glorification.

"For it is God who works in you both to will and to do for His good pleasure" (Phil. 2:13).

While we still have an old sin nature, though Satan is opposing us every step of the way, we must grow in the grace and knowledge of the Lord Jesus. It is also true that our entire life is different! If we are what we've always been, we are not saved. I know that I am saved because on the seventh of May, 1974, I received the Lord Jesus Christ as my Savior and also because I have never gotten over it! And it is not that we are trying to be saved. If I asked you, "Are you an elephant?" You would not say, "Well, I'm trying to be!" You either are an elephant or you're not. No one who is trying to be saved understands salvation. *You are either saved or you're not!* You are saved because you have had a personal, life-changing encounter with the Lord Jesus Christ at a point in time. It is a matter of trusting not trying.

So Are You Ready to Be Saved?

If this is something you want to do, then here is a suggested prayer; the words are not what's important but what's in your heart. If God is dealing with you, then cry out to Him:

Lord Jesus, I need you. Thank you for dying on the cross for my sins. I cannot save myself. I cannot even help you save me. But the best I know how, I confess that I am a sinner and believe that the Lord Jesus Christ died on the cross for my sins and rose from the dead. I open the door of my life and receive you right now as my Savior. Come in and make me the kind of person you want me to be.

If you just received the Lord Jesus Christ as your Savior, then you are saved! This promise is based on the authority of God's Word.

"But as many as received Him, to them He gave the right to become children of God, to those who believe in His name" (John 1:12).

A list of my other books: Go to Amazon.com and type in Johnny A Palmer Jr.

Genesis: Roots of the Nation Vol. 1
Genesis: Roots of the Nation Vol. 2
Genesis: Roots of the Nation Vol. 3
Exodus: Redemption of the Nation. Vol. 1
Exodus: Redemption of the Nation. Vol. 2
Book of Leviticus
Book of Numbers
Book of Deuteronomy
Book of Judges
First Samuel
Second Samuel
Book of Job
Psalms – Vol. 1, 2, 3
Jonah, God of the Second Chance
Nahum, the God who is good and angry
The Gospel of Mark: the servant.
The Gospel of Luke Vol. 1
The Gospel of Luke Vol. 2

The Gospel of Luke Vol. 3
The Gospel of Luke Vol. 4
The Gospel of John.
The Book of Acts
Ephesians: A Manual for Survival
Philippians – A Convoy of Joy.
1 Peter
2 Peter
Jude: Hey Jude
Revelation: The Revelation of Jesus Christ
A Manual for Revival
Practical Principles for Studying the Bible
Read Limit 30 mph
Proclamations from a Politically Incorrect Prophet
Elvis Wellness
Awake for the Dawn is About to Break
Rewards of Rejecting Christ
Which Messiah will you Meet?
GPS-23
Spiritual Survivor Man
A Father's Day Message
A Mother's Day Message
I'm For Life
Double Solitaire with the Trinity
Fuel – The Lord's Prayer
Back to the Basics

www.ingramcontent.com/pod-product-compliance
Lightning Source LLC
Chambersburg PA
CBHW030304030426
42337CB00012B/579